Love, Then Listen is the right advice for all parents of LGBTQ kids. Daphne Reiley's heartwarming book about her journey to "love, then listen" with her own child is essential reading for all parents who find themselves on a journey they never expected. Highly recommended!

Rev. Dr. David P. Gushee
Distinguished University Professor of
Christian Ethics
Director, Center for Theology & Public Life,
Mercer University
President, American Academy of Religion
Former President, Society of Christian Ethics

An extremely important book for parents struggling to reconcile their faith and their child's transgender identity. When religious beliefs are at odds with the child's gender identity it can be painful for the entire family. Parents often find themselves confused and grieving. During this time, finding strength in one's faith is vital. Author Daphne Reiley lights the way in this incredibly powerful, personal, and inspiring spiritual journey.

Kristine Medea, LPC, BCETS
Executive Director and Founder, TransThriving:
Therapeutic Wellness Program for
Gender Diverse Youth & Families

What delights me most about this
does not contain. Daphne Reiley, Fe
of their family did not experience re
church. Ministers, elders, and other ch
read this book! Read it because the
honesty, vulnerability, and love this
should be your model when a family ir
faces this reality. Be ready to love and lis

Rev. (
Christian Church (Discip

Love, Then Listen

❧

Sharing My Son's Journey
Toward His True Gender

DAPHNE C. REILEY

ISBN 978-1-63528-043-2

Printed in the United States of America

Cover Image by Sveta615

Reiley, Daphne C.

Love, Then Listen:
Sharing My Son's Journey Toward His True Gender

First Edition

Categories: Transgenderism, Religion/Spirituality

In gratitude for the grace, love, and compassion of God on a journey such as this.

To Ralph for his steadfast love, support, and companionship on this trek, without which I would have been lost.

To Thomas for his quiet understanding.

To Felix, with much love and with deep admiration of the man he is revealing.

DCR

Table of Contents

Acknowledgments

This book could not have been written without my faith; my husband, Ralph; our children, Thomas and Felix; our therapist, Kristine Medea, MA, LPC, BCETS; my employer, Victoria L. Collier, CELA; our circle of support, including friends, extended family, pastors, school administrators, teachers, doctors—this list could go on for quite a while!

My acknowledgments would be remiss if I didn't give immense credit to the editors who have helped me sculpt this memoir, affirmed my storytelling, and encouraged me to keep at it. Thank you to Victoria L. Collier, the Rev. Dr. James Brewer-Calvert, and the Rev. Dr. Joseph V. LaGuardia for your editorial expertise!

Simple thanks cannot express how our family experiences this support. Each of us, I am sure, experiences the support in different ways, to different depths. Yet, without this support, none of us would be where we are on this path.

The simple truth is that our child could very well not be here with us. That truth is the reason for this book.

Foreword

For all the good they accomplished, in 1611 the translators of the Authorized King James Version of the Bible did the parents of the world a great disservice—a disservice that has continued for over four centuries. Somewhere along the translation path, one of the forty-seven scholars from the Church of England perused the Hebrew and Aramaic texts of the Old Testament and decided the best rendering of Proverbs 22:6 was, "Train up a child in the way he should go, and when he is old, he will not depart from it." Thus, the guilt-ridden parent was born.

Training became our primary activity as parents. We taught—in a calm, patient, instructive, loving voice at first, but one that quickly escalated into screaming if rational decibel levels were ineffective. We disciplined and pushed and pulled and punished. We put our kids in a corner, across our laps for a spanking, in all the right schools, sometimes in reform schools, in therapy, and of course in church. We knew the way they "should go," and we were determined to do it right.

But, alas, our children grew. And more often than not, some portion of their life—if not all of their life—went contrary to where we thought they should go and who we thought they should be. The inevitable guilt of having parented poorly flooded upon us because our child "departed from the way he should go." Prayers followed. We prayed God would somehow correct what we had done wrong. We prayed God would usher our child back to the way we thought he should go. Those damn translators of the Authorized King James Version of the Bible—if they had gotten this one verse right, they might have saved us a ton of grief and guilt.

Daphne Reiley gets it right. The Hebrew phrase embedded in Proverbs 22:6 can be transliterated *al pi darkow*. The best understanding of this phrase is not "the way he should go," but "the way he is bent." If we train up our children in the way they are naturally bent, they will not depart from it. Why? Because this is who they are! This is who they are created to be! Children are not bonsai trees to be twisted and wired and stunted into unintended shapes and forms. They are creations of God. And when we nurture their natural bends, they do not depart from it. The only way to do this well is to do more listening than yelling.

The only thing harder than parenting is processing theology while you parent. Again, Daphne Reiley gets it right. Daphne—more from necessity than scholarly curiosity—brings her keen theological training and insight to these chapters of her life. She not only learns to listen to her child and allow that child to become the blessed creation God intended, but she also learns to listen to God. Her gift to us is her story. Her holy attentiveness through this journey provides a treasure trove for the rest of us. She helps us learn to listen. And in our listening we come to love our children, as well as all of God's children, for who they are created to be.

Dr. Jim Dant
Senior Minister, First Baptist Church,
Greenville, South Carolina

Change can bring your life into focus.

Seen on the FOCUS Insurance street sign,
Lawrenceville Highway, Decatur, Georgia

Introduction

This book is as much a product of what I have perceived as my failures as that of my successes. Of course, that's all relative. I want to share both failures and successes in hopes of putting a human as well as a divine face on someone doing her best to love and support a child moving through such a transition.

The thoughts that flooded into my heart and head when our son first shared his reality with us could not have been counted. After the initial shock, I immediately began wondering just how long he had known this about himself and how I could have missed it!

So many questions, so few answers.

As we have traveled this path with our child since the Fall of 2014, some of those questions have been answered—they've had to be, because there were new questions waiting.

I will be sharing my experience of this transition as the mother who gave birth to this beautiful, brave, and wondrous child.

My hope is that by sharing my experience, the door will be opened to many other mothers to accept and not fear accompanying their child on this journey with love, grace, and respect. As mothers we are purveyors of grace for our children. We are conduits of God's grace and mercy. Through our unconditional love we can move with our children as they find and reveal themselves, all the while easing their fears.

I share my experiences with this transition because I know there are others out there who might be needing some hope, some understanding, and some way of finding their faith in the midst of such a transition.

It is important at this point to make my belief clear on the subject of sin as it may relate to matters of transgenderism. This book is not in any way about "loving the sinner, hating the sin." This book is all about allowing the mothering, nurturing love of God to support our child and ourselves as our child moves through the phases of transitioning. There is no sin here.

Throughout the book I will refer to my child by his correct name—Felix. Part of my story revolves around setting aside my expectations for a daughter, which Felix bore with grace. Now that I am aware Felix was there all along, I can more easily think of and refer to him all the time—even in sharing memories—as Felix. I realize this may be confusing at times when I am sharing memories from his youth.

One final note: you will find at the beginning of each chapter a verse of Scripture or a quotation (or perhaps both) that has spoken to me as I have moved through this process. I may or may not address the connection within the chapter; I feel safe in allowing you, the reader, to draw those conclusions.

I praise you,

for I am fearfully and wonderfully made.

Wonderful are your works;

that I know very well.

Psalm 139:14

The Beginning:
Listening, Really Listening

The last week had been difficult for our entire family. I had brought Felix to a follow-up session with his therapist and was settled down to read a magazine in the waiting room. The therapist opened her door and asked that I come in, saying Felix had something he wanted to tell me.

As soon as I entered the room, I felt excitement and a sort of delight pulsing from my child!

I took my seat next to Felix and gave him a smile and a hug. We were sitting close together when Felix drew back and away from me a bit. I turned to look at him as he said, "Mom, I'm a boy." It felt like the entire room froze, that my heart froze, that my head stopped.

Those were hard, flinty words for me to hear as the mother of a beautiful child whom I knew as a girl.

So many thoughts roared through my head, ranging from "What!?" to "How can this be? I'm so confused." Felix's words would change my heart and my vision of our world forever. Those words set off an explosion of grief. As Felix found his voice and shared this truth for the first time with me, I was so thankful we were with our therapist!

In that very short but endlessly long moment, what came over me was a sudden peace and stillness. I should have recognized it right then since I have had similar experiences in other instances of receiving heart-changing, mind-changing news. God showed up, big time!

Through the grace of God, the first words I uttered were, "I love you; you are fearfully and wonderfully made." These words arose in my heart, I think, as much for my own benefit as for that of my child. These words, I hope, told Felix we would not abandon him or stop loving him. These words revealed to us both that God is in this with us.

I remember that just as Felix had drawn away from me to share his truth, we now came together, and perhaps because of my fear of losing him, I held him tightly. We each shed our share of tears—but shared in the weeping. He revealed more about what this had meant for him, that the fear he felt about not understanding himself was part of the reason for his cutting. Before my eyes Felix revealed the beginnings of his transition. There was a newfound strength visible, a confidence in knowing himself more honestly.

There was a delight in his eyes—a delight, I'm sure, arising from being true to who he is.

There was also a shade to his eyes betraying his tentative acceptance of my reassurance of our continued full love for him.

As our family has stepped upon this path, we have stumbled; we have been angry; we have grieved; we have not understood. There have been times when I've felt as though the rug has been pulled from under my feet. As a result of my grief and my lack of understanding, I've felt as though Felix has become a stranger to me. There have also been beautiful, fun, crazy moments when I look at Felix and simply smile. I smile because it is so obvious he is moving toward wholeness and happiness. In October 2015 we celebrated Felix's first birthday with a party and a special cake! The party was a celebration of our family's passage from what was to what is—a celebration of realizations (because they kept rolling in over that first year).

As shell-shocked as my heart and head have been, my spirit has been calm.

That calmness is where I experience God in all of this. I know God's presence concretely. The words I shared with Felix are from Psalm 139—one of my favorites. Over the years I have found the Psalms to be a gift of words and images that have comforted and directed me during difficult, confusing times by bringing my thoughts, my worries, and my fears into the light of God's love. I have held on to the words "for I am fearfully and wonderfully made" throughout my own life. When I consider that God has made me fearfully and wonderfully, I believe I am capable of handling whatever comes my way. So it is not surprising that these words bring me to a place of faith and feelings of peace and trust during a challenging period in our family's life.

We will be okay.

Felix and I have had many talks about how he's doing and how I'm doing with this transition. Thankfully, he has been open to hear my thoughts, which obviously concern him, even to the point of correction or argument on his part. That said, although impatient with my slip-ups as to name and pronouns, I believe Felix understands on some level how difficult it has been for me to give up my vision of him as my daughter. My belief in his compassion keeps me working on my own part in this transition. During one of our talks, I told Felix I don't believe God makes mistakes. Only now do I realize he may have heard what I said in a way that was confusing and perhaps hurtful. An honest admission would be that I said it without really thinking, without filtering first through thoughts of how Felix would hear it— reacting to my own doubts in the moment more than from a place of supporting Felix.

What I meant is that I have experienced God as our creator—we are beautiful and good; we are all a reflection of God; we are fearfully and wonderfully made. Just as we have been created, so we are beloved. Whatever the manner in which we are put together, whatever we look like, however we experience ourselves—in regard to gender, sexuality, etc.—our moral worth is centered in the love and light of God we carry within us and share with the world. We have been created to be revealed by our faith, and the quality of our faith has nothing to do with our bodies. We are revealed by our faith when we live as we are meant to live—full of that love and light of God within us. In all the variety of beautiful creation, how can we limit the human body to such a narrow, binary understanding? How do we dare attempt to limit the beauty of God's love and light? I have the faith and the experience that God is with us wherever we find ourselves, as we find ourselves. As we draw nearer to God, we are drawn nearer to our own truth. The grace that Felix continues to show is only possible because it comes from God.

Although both of my sons have participated in church with me within our faith community of First Christian Church of Decatur, Felix has shied away over the last few years. He is uncomfortable being in a group of people who "knew him when he was a kid." When he shared that with me, I understood the implications. However, I reminded him that of all places, Decatur First would love and accept him. Still, for now, Felix doesn't attend church with me. I ask him to go as a matter of checking in at times; however, he remains aloof. I'm not sure if he knows and/or understands what he believes right now spiritually, which kind of makes sense in part given the transition he is moving through. I do know that he is aware of God and God's presence. Felix is very aware of what I do in terms of my spiritual life in community and in private. He knows I pray, constantly, for our family, others we know, and many we don't. I do know that he prays—even if he doesn't acknowledge that what he's doing is prayer.

Not long ago, while at school, he realized he had not brought something with him that he needed. In a show of Spirit, he later shared with me that he had hoped "God was going to show up for him" in that situation. I asked him when he had been doing this. Felix's response made me shiver. At the same time Felix had been "hoping" God would show up, I had felt the overwhelming, urgent need to pray while at work. My prayer—my demand—was that God show up for Felix. I was fervently praying for something God already knew—that Felix needed God to make God's presence known. I did not know why, but I knew God did. This instance was not a plea on my part; it was the pure demand of a mother for her child.

As sure as I know God is in this, I know God has provided a sense of presence for Felix. That presence—that grace—is a big part of the golden thread that will keep Felix together when he feels like falling apart; it will sustain him when he finds himself exhausted emotionally, physically, and spiritually.

Grace is deep within us—a part of the mystery of our creation, of the inhabiting of our bodies by the soul God has given us.

Grace is our measured breath, our pause, our curiosity, and our strength.

We all have been given the grace with which to encounter the fear we have of anything we perceive as different. Fear is taught to us by those to whom we look for knowledge and understanding. Unfortunately, oftentimes, this education has been at the hands of organized religion. "Church" has done grave damage to those in the world who love, live, and perceive themselves in ways that might be strange to us.

In learning more about transgenderism, I understand the condition is one that has been present all along within the population in some discernible percentage. How society has dealt with the dysphoria of transgenderism has varied over the millennia; however, rarely has it been treated with lovingkindness, understanding, and acceptance. The one exception of which I have learned is that of Native Americans who have a name for people who were born into one body yet experienced themselves as another gender. It's something like "two spirits," which really makes sense to me. In their society, in their interactions with community, these "two-spirit" individuals were simply accepted as the complex beings we all are. Oh, how wonderful if all of us could be that understanding and loving!

Society's expectations and understandings of what we should act like and look like are so very binary. I often wonder if we all simply accepted the way God has made us—good, beautiful, and complex—would we see the divinity within each of us? Would we be so caught up in how we each looked? Whom we each loved? How we each experienced ourselves along the spectrum of gender?

Our coming together in the womb, covered by the mysteries of God, is just that—a coming together impervious to scrutiny by science and human understanding. I feel it deep within me that there are aspects to our formation that are mysterious, that are a function of the divine creative force within us, and totally beyond our control and understanding.

That said, I am grateful that our scientific and social understandings have grown and that we see physical anomalies presented at birth more clinically and understand those anomalies are caused by external factors—not as punishments paid out by an angry, vengeful God.

To those in our midst who believe gender nonconformity is some type of birth defect, I urge you to give thought to the discoveries made by geneticists, developmental psychiatrists, and psychologists that have proven otherwise. It is possible to be born with female chromosomes and male genitalia (or vice versa). Further brain research has revealed that it is indeed possible to be born with female genitalia and female chromosomes but a male brain.[1] Transgenderism is now a recognized diagnosis approved to receive appropriate medical intervention and treatment in order to alleviate the dysphoria within patients. Medical interventions and treatments include hormone replacement therapies as well as commensurate surgeries.

Unfortunately, a great part of the population has yet to differentiate and understand the complexities of the development of self-perception and how that is determined and grows as we develop as individuals. The development of our brain is still part of that miraculous coming together in a fearfully and wonderfully powerful way: "Our anatomy, chromosomes and brain cells all correspond as either male or female. But some people are born with variations in one or two of these indicators."[2] Additionally, "according to medical science, chromosomal variances occur within moments of conception, and anatomical development happens within the nine months in the womb."[3]

How we perceive ourselves as far as gender is concerned is a beautiful, complex gift of God—and it is not bound to the genitals we possess at birth.

Endnotes

[1] Mark Wingfield, "Seven Things I'm Learning About Transgender Persons," *Baptist News Global*, opinion, May 13, 2016.

[2] Ibid.

[3] Ibid.

Questions for Consideration

1. Consider how your faith has supported you through difficult events in your life. Share a particular time when you were afraid but calm because of your faith.

2. Have you ever been faced with an event in your life in which you had little to no input yet were expected to come to some level of acceptance?

   a. How did your faith sustain you in the beginning?

   b. How did your faith carry you through the changes in heart, in knowing, in loving into which this event led you?

3. What is your basic understanding of transgenderism? Has it changed?

Come to me, all you that are weary and are carrying heavy burdens, and I will give you rest. Take my yoke upon you, and learn from me; for I am gentle and humble in heart, and you will find rest for your souls. For my yoke is easy, and my burden is light.

Matthew 11:28–30

The Prequel:
Intuition

Thanksgiving 2000. Thoughts of turkey and dressing and all the trimmings made me want to throw up! I was nearing 40. Our son Thomas wasn't quite three years old, and we were older parents. Thomas had been an easy, wonderful baby and toddler. Admittedly, I wasn't too sure I wanted to take a chance on having another baby.

My mom was hosting Thanksgiving. I called and told her I wasn't feeling too well and that the thoughts of the traditional Thanksgiving meal didn't get me excited. She suggested we have meatballs and spaghetti instead. That worked. We had a pretty good turkeyless Turkey Day eating our Italian supper!

At some point leading up to Turkey Day, I realized I was fine during the day, but in the mornings I felt awful. In considering this information, Ralph and I thought we needed to rule out my being pregnant and possibly get a doctor's appointment. The morning after Thanksgiving, we went to CVS and bought two pregnancy tests (different brands) and went home.

I sat waiting, feeling so afraid, so caught by surprise.

There it was—a line on both telling me I was pregnant. Ralph and I looked at each other and wondered what to do. We didn't tell anyone; after all, at my age things could be going wrong to fool my body into thinking it was pregnant, right? (I realize this is a mighty sign of denial. No argument there!) I made a doctor's appointment and remember being extremely nervous going into the doctor's office, giving the nurse a urine sample, and getting ready for the examination. The doctor came in and confirmed I was pregnant. My due date was July 27, 2001.

The ride home from that doctor's appointment was very still, very quiet. Ralph had met me at the doctor's office and returned to work. I returned to our home, alone.

Grace.

In our neighborhood we had a wonderful old Italian grandma who lived across the street from us. She had loved our family since we moved into the neighborhood. Quite frequently, our son Thomas ran over to her house to say hello. Grace, her name, also defined her way of being. Grace had been telling me frequently (read gentle, loving nagging) that I should have another child, that Thomas didn't need to be an only child, that Thomas needed a built-in playmate. I was well aware that Grace prayed. She was a good Catholic. Without telling her what sort of doctor, I had asked her to keep Thomas for me while I went for my appointment.

I returned from the doctor's visit, parked the car in our driveway, and breathed deeply before I slowly walked over to Grace's. I was in shock. I was thinking of what we were going to do now. Making my way down Grace's driveway, littered with leaves, wearing a short-sleeve shirt due to it being a beautiful, warm autumn that year, the evidence of bloodwork was revealed. Grace may have been in her late 70s, yet she was very observant. She came to the door with Thomas, and her eyes went immediately to the bandage. She asked if everything was okay. I said, "Yes, and thank you for keeping Thomas." I took Thomas's hand, and we took our time walking up the driveway. Stopping near the end, I turned and looked back. Grace was still standing there, watching me, concern clearly showing in her eyes. I called to her that she had her wish. I said nothing else, turned around once more, and kept walking. After just a few steps, I heard her cry out and laugh, "That baby's mine all right! I'm claiming it." Claim it she did. Her wish or her prayer—either one—had been handily answered. Grace always loved Thomas, yet this child was hers.

Since I was pregnant again, I decided another boy would be easy. I felt like I knew (at least anatomically) how to care for a boy. Funny how I thought I had any input on that! To add a wrinkle, because I was a mother of "advanced maternal age" (sigh), my obstetrician required that I undergo amniocentesis. Ralph and I went for the test, hoping for an all clear yet agreeing that even if something came up, we would still love this child. I had shared with Ralph my desire for another boy; he had remained quiet. We also had agreed that we didn't want to know the gender of this baby—we hadn't known when we had Thomas and found it exciting.

A few days later, I was standing just outside our front door when the phone rang. The nurse was calling me to relay the amnio results. She happily confirmed all signs were great. She then told me that everything indicated we were going to have a healthy baby girl. I must have sucked in my breath because the nurse reacted by offering an apology for telling me the gender.

Within my mother's heart, accepting the fact that we were going to have a girl, I also began dreaming of "girly" things—proms, weddings, babies. A recent admission to my therapist of my earliest feelings around gender led her to suggest that I could perhaps look at it as an intuitive knowing—that the baby I carried was a boy. At this point I am choosing to keep that thought close to my heart. Holding on to good, positive, loving thoughts has been an important aspect of our transition as a family and has gotten us through some tough times. Those good, positive, loving thoughts are all part of a golden thread of God's grace.

The baby came out several days early, hungry for life, nursing in the delivery room for 45 minutes!

He grew and developed into a beautiful child. A beautiful "wild" child who only wanted to play with his brother and his brother's friends. A child who didn't like wearing clothes, who enjoyed his body and the freedom he had. One beautiful day, I looked out the kitchen window to behold my children peeing upon the giant oak tree in our backyard. Now, Thomas most likely thought our neighbors couldn't see what they were doing. What he hadn't calculated was the fact that anyone looking out the kitchen window could. What ensued was a rather hilarious scene of Felix trying his best to pee outside like his brother but failing. He was so disappointed and demanded an explanation. Thinking of that conversation so long ago speaks of foreshadowing, perhaps even an inner knowing of my own.

I remember explaining why he couldn't: "You don't have the same equipment as your brother."

Felix loved romping and climbing trees and doing everything Thomas did. Every time I saw the two of them together, I smiled because they were so alike in so many ways. In fact, they were often mistaken for twins because of their "cotton-top" blond hair, fair skin, and similar heights. Both of my children were (and still are) beautiful!

Scrubbing green oil-based paint off this determined child because Felix wanted to be the Hulk was hilarious. I was so very happy that my friend Eve was here visiting that particular day and that she is a trained esthetician. Color and artistic process have continued to this day. Luckily, I think, creativity now more often shows itself with hair color, not oil-based paint!

While for both boys tree climbing, getting dirty, and playing Army were popular, so were cooking in the play kitchen and dancing. I have beautiful memories of watching Thomas teach his brother how to climb our dogwood in the front yard. It's a perfect beginner tree, easily accessible. So patient. (Thomas enjoys showing others how to do things; I'll be watching to see how he uses that gift later in his life.)

Never was there a purposeful gender division between what Thomas could/should do and what Felix could/should do. There were differences in the way they thought—without a doubt. There were differences in what Thomas and Felix enjoyed overall. Underlying all their togetherness was a definite feeling that Felix could not understand why he couldn't do everything Thomas was doing—never mind that he was three years younger! In my eyes and in my heart, the age difference was the only difference truly irreconcilable. Halloweens were spent being some boyish character; Halloweens were spent being some girlish character. It all seems, in retrospect, to be experimentation or, perhaps, simply a child playing and being comfortable with all the parts of who he is.

From his birth we never really cut Felix's hair. When he was about three or four, he began wanting his hair in multiple braids—not one or two, but usually five or seven (always an odd number). He always ended up looking like a wild child with golden braids flying. Felix was his own self. At one point his hair was way below his waist. Beautiful hair— yet if we didn't keep it brushed, it would end up in a horrible tangle underneath. In fact, at one point I came home from being away for a couple days to find his hair totally caught up. There was no way of getting it untangled, so cutting it off was our only option, resulting in tears from both of us. After that, Felix had a cute little golden-blond bob for a while, but his hair never grew out as long again.

Felix and Ralph began violin lessons together when he was five and Ralph was fifty. I loved watching the two of them go off to violin lessons. These lessons were something that provided time together as well as a bit of "competitiveness" between Ralph and Felix. Most often, their teachers held their recitals at area assisted-living facilities and once at our church, First Christian Church of Decatur. Fortunately, most of the time, neither teacher required Felix to "dress" up.

At the age of 10 or 11, Felix became interested in learning piano so he could learn how to play some of his favorite music. (As I was writing this, I asked Felix if I could share the music he had so wanted to learn—alas, he has forbidden me to say!) Felix began learning to play the piano in a more traditional manner, but then transitioned to a teacher who taught using the Suzuki method. Once Felix began the Suzuki method, he found the lessons challenging. I marveled at how Felix excelled at both violin and piano because he enjoyed the challenge. At one point, when I offered to let him drop one of the instruments, he responded, "Why would I want to do that? The violin is so hard, the piano gives my brain a rest." I was floored!

Close to Christmas in eighth grade, His Suzuki teacher began speaking with Felix about participating in the yearly Suzuki Association's recital at Spivey Hall. This recital required the participants to perform in evening attire. At this point Felix had come out to us; however, we were only very inexpertly and slowly communicating this to folks. A sweet, private conversation with his piano teacher revealed she was fine with him finding an appropriate tuxedo. A tremendous weight of stress was alleviated for all of us. Unfortunately, for reasons beyond our control, the recital never happened. As the new year of lessons started, Felix refused to continue. I was, and still am, sad about that decision. I never was successful at teasing out a reason. The piano, however, had been his choice to take up, not ours. Yet now that middle school orchestra is in the past, the violin sits in the case; the piano sits in the music room. For some reason I am confident they will be played again.

Questions for Consideration

1. If you have more than one child, have you found yourself comparing your children? Drawing conclusions about their futures based upon their genders?

2. What expectations do you have for your son or your daughter? Are they different?

3. Where do you experience God in these expectations?

God is our refuge and strength,
a very present help in trouble.

~

Be still, and know that I am God!

Psalm 46:1, 10

Listening to My Own Heart

When I think of these experiences, I wonder if I kept a sort of record in my head and heart of the ways in which Felix was attempting to figure himself out. In fact, several months into the transition, Felix asked, "Mom, remember when I wouldn't wear anything but skorts the first semester of sixth grade? I was doing my best, Mom, to be a girl. I really was."

When he shared this, my heart broke a little more.

This intelligent, beautiful person was struggling on his own to be what his body suggested him to be and thus what the world expected him to be. How I wish he could have confided in me then.

I have wondered for a long time why Felix felt he couldn't confide in me. I have been concerned it was because he didn't know what our reaction would be and was scared we would stop loving him. The emotions that surface when I think that could possibly be why are not pretty: fear, worry, even anger. These emotions surface because I can't believe Felix doesn't know how much we love him—and what that means.

God knit Felix together in my womb and knows just how special he is, knows what his path is, knows his thoughts before he thinks them—much less before they reach his mouth. I see this over and over. Felix is an avid researcher, full of curiosity and a burning need to know and understand. He only recently shared with me that the information and feedback he received in online chat rooms and Tumblr and Snapchat were exactly why he had never shared this with us. He "knew"—but he really wasn't certain—we would accept and continue to love him. When Felix told me that, I realized he was only 11 or 12 at the time he was freshly exploring his feelings and his perceptions of himself. I thought about my own inner life at that age and concluded I would not have told my parents either.

In fifth grade Felix began dressing in large clothing, obviously hiding the body he had previously enjoyed. The refusal to wear dresses—ever—was not a totally bad thing in my book. Yet at his promotion ceremony, I blindly adhered to the dresses for girls "rule." I failed to advocate for Felix and get a clarification about whether dress pants would suffice. Shopping for a dress for that occasion turned out to be a beautiful experience for us as mother and child.

It was as though Felix, in a gesture of acceptance of the inevitable, had decided to make it as enjoyable as possible. I on the other hand had been dreading it!

As Felix and I began looking at dresses, he would pull one out and present it to me as a possibility, knowing full well I would be revolted. Then I started pulling out an outfit and bringing it to him for approval. Well, you can guess—Felix would start laughing. This attitude, full of grace and compassion on Felix's part, made this experience tolerable. When I saw Felix at the ceremony, he had on the dress we had finally settled on while shopping together, but he was wearing his high-tops. Well, to be perfectly honest, we had not really discussed shoes!

Of course, as I have been thinking about the early parts of Felix's journey, I am so convicted! Even though we had never denied Felix the opportunities that were considered "boyish," I enjoyed seeing my child in a dress once in a while—even when doing so obviously distressed him. The instance of his promotion ceremony was an opportunity for me to force the issue and insist on his wearing a dress. I remember flashing anger hitting me when I saw the high-tops. First, I was angry at my husband for allowing Felix to wear them. Secondly, I was angry at

Felix for being so insistent about such a thing. Only later did my guilt begin as I realized I hadn't truly wanted Felix to be able to wear something other than a dress, so I hadn't advocated for the possibility.

The large, baggy clothes Felix was wearing most of the time seemed to be a sign that he wasn't happy with his body, which I actually thought to be fairly normal at that age. Felix was developing early; his body was changing. Now I realize just how hurtful, frightening, and confusing that all had to be. Still no confiding, still no sharing—even with some gentle nagging.

At the end of seventh grade, we found out Felix had been cutting. A couple months before this discovery, Felix had begun isolating himself in his room—going so far as making an actual nest for himself with blankets and pillows where he could hide. Thomas heard Felix crying one night and went in to find him in this nest, with cuts visible on his legs. This discovery began our family's long journey to the reveal.

At the time cutting was a scary, clique-y thing happening among fifth- and sixth-grade girls. As we later learned, after being "introduced" to cutting by some of his friends, cutting for Felix became about attempting to find a way of releasing the anger, fear, and tension that vibrated through him. When Felix was stressed out about school or social interactions, that anger and fear would come to a head, resulting in cutting.

I was confused, terrified, angry, and totally unprepared to handle the situation.

My heartache grew.

I could not understand what was wrong.

I couldn't get Felix to open up and talk. Besides being heartbroken I was so scared by my lack of comprehension and knowledge. The question that kept swirling through my head was, "Why didn't I know?" During an intervention appointment with his psychologist, Felix promised us all that he would quit, that he would instead come to us.

We removed access to all of the scissors and knives in the house that we could find. What was sickening to me was that Felix could always find something: paper clips, tweezers, things we never considered a risk. The process of attempting to eliminate possibilities was terrifying to a degree because I knew just how intelligent and creative my child was!

That entire summer, we kept our promise to be available—whenever and however he needed us to be. While we kept our end of the bargain, Felix rarely reached out and told us he was afraid, angry, sad, disappointed, anything. Yet over Labor Day weekend as we flew out to Denver to see some friends, I discovered fresh cuts. It was as though he really wanted to be discovered—wearing shorts that rode up as he sat on the plane. That weekend was very difficult. To say that I was extremely angry with Felix is an understatement. *Fury* would be a better word—anger wrapped up with fear, frustration, guilt. I explained to Felix that he had broken his promise to us, that we had been available and open to hearing whatever he had to say—to simply be with him when he was feeling bad—but he had not taken advantage of our presence.

I felt cut. I felt shut out. I was scared.

When we returned home, only a few weeks passed before we had to admit Felix to a psychiatric, behavioral hospital—one of the most difficult decisions we as parents ever have had to make. Felix had said he was thinking of suicide. We had to keep him safe.

What was wrong? Why couldn't I figure this out?

I was so frightened and clearly didn't understand why this was happening. I was screaming at and to God for some understanding, some help with this child—God's child.

Taking our child to such a place brought up memories of taking my mom to a dementia care facility and leaving her there. I experienced the same guilt. Felix was fine and understood he needed the help (there's that grace again). Yet after moving Felix and ourselves through the emotionally overwhelming process of admitting him, we were told he had to have other shoes. So we returned to the house and went back with the allowable shoes. I went in and asked at the desk about getting the shoes to Felix. They were very nonchalant about it and let me go back into the locked area since it was the formal visiting time. I met Felix in the day room where other kids were being visited by their families. We sat across from each other in orange plastic chairs. In just one hour he seemed a bit crazed, giving me reasons why I should take him home, swearing he didn't belong there, promising he would stop hurting himself. To my "mother's eyes" Felix was obviously scared.

I had to explain to Felix that I understood he was scared, yet I also understood he did indeed need to be there for his own safety, for his own time to work out what was going on, whatever he needed to figure out. I hugged him and left. I was in agony when I left. I felt I had abandoned my child in a place where he could easily get hurt, where he would be made to do some deep digging. I knew how scary that could be. I wanted to run back and get Felix, but I didn't. I knew I had to trust the doctors to help him make some sense of his own pain and anger.

Felix was there for a week—a very long week for all of us.

When we were finally allowed to come and get Felix, he was changed. He spoke of friends made, of the harsh conditions. When he had been admitted, I had briefly seen the bedrooms; they seemed dark and dreary.

Friends. My heart clutched at that word. Kids just as broken, or worse, were Felix's friends now. Thoughts rose of not wanting Felix to have those friends. This intelligent, gentle child had survived "that place."

I kept Felix close for the weekend, very close. I wanted to hold on to him.

As close as I wanted to keep him, Felix seemed to hold himself aloof, in a different way than before, like he was holding tight to something. This change puzzled me. We still cuddled on the couch. Yet, not surprisingly, Felix didn't really seem to want to talk much about what had happened at the hospital.

As a requirement of his discharge, Felix had to have a follow-up appointment with his therapist within three or four days. So the following week I took him for that appointment. I had just settled in to read a magazine in the lobby when the therapist poked her head out of the door and asked me to come in. When I entered the room, Felix was sitting on the couch, and I went to sit down next to him. She said Felix had something he needed to tell me.

I prepared myself, so I thought, to hear whatever had to be said.

Questions for Consideration

1. Have you ever worried about the mental state of a child—yours or someone else's? What has been your response?

2. Was your faith your guide? How so?

3. How did your faith give you hope in your experience?

Compassion, kindness, respect, and understanding is the golden thread that keeps us together.

Peter J. Karlsson.

You shall love the Lord your God with all your heart, and with all your soul, and with all your mind. This is the greatest and first commandment. And a second is like it: You shall love your neighbor as yourself. On these two commandments hang all the law and the prophets.

Matthew 22:37–40

Golden Threads

The "golden thread" is an image of the invisible, ever-present, unending grace of God. Grace winds its way through all our lives—no matter what, a gift of God.

Walter Brueggemann, an eminent Old Testament theologian and scholar, once taught a class I attended on Isaiah. During the class Brueggemann introduced to us the idea of orientation, disorientation, and reorientation as distinct periods of our lives that are often repeated. He explained that as we grow in our faith, we are moving along, accepting the way things are, and understanding what we understand; we are oriented. At some point along that trail, we experience something—physically, emotionally, spiritually (or all three)—that knocks us out of our safe feeling of orientation; we are disoriented. This period is rich in possibility for the development of our faith, for our growth toward God, toward a greater understanding of that relationship. As we move through the period of disorientation, we (hopefully) slowly move into a time of reorientation. At this point Brueggemann offers a caveat: this realization of reorientation can be misleading. Reorientation often bears striking resemblance to the time before disorientation. However, it is important to stop and reflect on the fruit of our time of disorientation. How have we changed, grown, matured? We were urged not to cheat ourselves out of reaping the fruit of that labor! So reorientation may be familiar, but it is not the same as before because we are not the same.

Any time we move through periods of disorientation in our lives, if we seek out and hold on to the golden threads within our experiences, we will soon have a secure rope to hold us, to guide us through to the other side: the reorientation of our lives, of our thoughts, even of our genders. The beauty is that God provides us those golden threads through God's pure grace, through God's presence during periods of disorientation.

In the months leading up to Felix finding his voice, he had been educating me—slowly but surely—about gender issues. Often this education brought up a sense of impatience in me. I was so unaware! So much for an awareness of moving into a period of disorientation. It's amusing now to look back at those conversations and realize just how much Felix was attempting to communicate in his own unique way—and realize just how dim I was! Often when Felix is working something out internally, he teaches me important details about whatever is cranking around in his head. Apparently, no matter how many times I had experienced Felix doing this, I never considered that what he was attempting to communicate was particular to his experience.

A summary of what I learned from Felix is that gender is in our head.

Gender is how we perceive ourselves as male or female, or a little bit of both, or neither; however, it is an individual's personal perception.

It is obvious where confusion can arise; for most people, their perception of their gender matches their physicality—or at least to such a point as to not produce a dysphoric experience.

With this transition I hurt deeply each time I realize just how disconnected Felix has become from his body. When he was little, he loved his body. I am sure that at some point he will come to accept—and even love—his body once again. I am hopeful in that I have seen some reorientation in that aspect of Felix's transition. What I most desire for Felix is an ease of being. The only way I see to nurture him in developing that sense of ease is to love him unconditionally and support him emotionally and physically as he explores what this means for him now and in the future.

Just as Felix has now become truly immersed in being the boy he is, so has his family. The transition for me has become similar to that of someone who becomes fluent in a second language. Eventually, one begins to think in that language when speaking it, not constantly translating from one language to the other. I have days when I don't even think about Felix as anything other than the boy he is. Part of any immersive experience is that of coming up and through to the other side. As I am writing this, I realize, with regard to pronouns and names, it has become easier for me to refer to Felix as Felix—even when talking about his birth—signaling a huge transition for me.

Undeniably, though, the transition is colored by grief, by a knowledge not capable of being "unknown." I simply cannot forget that I had a daughter for 13 years. However, I can choose to immerse myself in this new language, this new way of being present for my child, and do my best never to waver. There are days, still, that I find myself oddly upset, lonely in a weird way. I realize I am still grieving. I have to ask the typical grief-stricken questions: "When will this be done? When will I be healed of this pain, this sense of loss?"

I've had enough experience in sitting with folks who are grieving to know that grief never really goes away—because the loss remains. The tremendous grace in this instance is that the loss is one of experience and expectations, not a physical loss of my child. The gratitude I feel for that fact lightens the grief I do experience. The grace is that my child is truly growing into himself just like our son Thomas has been doing.

Felix and I have had many opportunities to spend some fun time together—out and about, laughing, just being easy with each other. Those times have made me so happy, hopeful, and thankful for the progress I've made in my heart. This journey is, and will continue to be, a learning experience for our family (and our many friends who support us).

God abundantly loves my child, does not condemn my child, and is present with my child. This belief more than justifies my love of my son. This heartfelt belief is a strand of the golden thread. I would help my child if he had been born with a cleft palate. The challenges to my child's development—

physical, emotional, and mental—could be seen as similar. The medical treatments he is now receiving to assist in his physical transition are equal to corrective surgery for a cleft palate. Fixing something that is not correct or that is dysphoric about one's body should not be looked at as wrong, as meddling with God's design for us. Nor should it be considered as taking away the cross that's been laid down for us, choosing not to pick it up. I've heard all these things. I am left with the reality that I don't need any justification for loving my child; the love I have for my child has been put there by God.

The work Felix has had to do emotionally and psychologically in order to be approved to receive any sort of physical, medical support in his transition has been immense and not lightly undertaken and will continue as long as he lives. As part of this work Felix has had to do, he has been fortunate to have Kristine Medea as his primary psychologist. Kristine is the founder of TransThriving, a program under the auspices of Thriving Heart Counseling. She has been working with trans youth and their families for years. Felix also regularly meets with a psychiatrist for medication management since he lives with depression (a genetic predisposition) and anxiety.

Recently, he has been able to reduce his medication for anxiety, I believe due in large part to the state of his transition at this point.

In seeking ways of preparing and sustaining Felix and our family for the journey we are undertaking, I keep being drawn to a passage from Micah that has been with me for years. It is deceptively simple—a message not buried within a parable or metaphor, a message that continues to be a powerful challenge to my life and the way I live it.

> He has told you, O mortal, what is good;
> and what does the LORD require of you
> but to do justice, and to love kindness, and
> to walk humbly with your God?

Loving kindness and practicing justice are difficult enough, but to do so with humility makes this passage especially difficult. Humility is defined as the quality or condition of being humble, and humble is defined as being marked by meekness or modesty in behavior, attitude, or spirit. Nowhere in this passage from Micah is passing judgment to be found. In fact, judgment of others simply cannot be done in true humility before God—another strand of the golden thread.

Social constructs lead us quite frequently to fear and thus judge that which does not fit into the categories we have accepted as true or good based upon ill-informed, ill-considered, and/or fear-based "knowledge." Our social constructs are informed by many aspects of life, including our faith traditions. How does this fear and judgment fit within the context of our being called as Christians to live our lives with lovingkindness and justice, to love God and others with humility?

Over the years much has changed with respect to bullying and discrimination. Within most schools there are policies in place enforcing a "no-bullying zone." To the extent that a school's administrative team enforces that policy, young people who are "not like everyone else" experience a deeper sense of safety and security in moving through that part of their lives. Unfortunately, even with teaching and leading by example, there remain young people who are susceptible to the poison of fear still existing within their parents' generation.

We still see anger and discrimination alive and well among young adults who have been brought up with the belief that not all people are worthy of respect, that not all people—especially those who look

differently, worship differently, or love differently—
are deserving of life itself. Chilling examples of that
sort of thinking have filled the news recently.

Yet our family's experiences have revealed that
many adolescents and teens now are more curious
and more willing to accept others as they are and
want to understand more and more about the friends
they have who are not exactly like themselves. Felix
tells me his social transition among his friends has
been remarkably smooth. Of course, his friends
had been calling him "Felix" since seventh grade!
Felix's friends are accepting of how Felix sees and
experiences himself—another strand of the golden
thread. Wow! Think about that for a moment. How
many adults have friendships like that?

My hope comes from my own observation that
we are in the midst of a generation growing up in
which such conduct is possible because families
live side by side with people who are different, who
worship differently, who clothe themselves differently,
who marry differently, who live differently. Our
world is no longer vanilla; we live in an environment
rich with outward and inward diversity. When our
family found our home, we were pleased to discover
the diversity of the neighborhood and the schools.

Having our children grow up in a neighborhood more accurately resembling the world into which they would move was high on our list of desires for a place to live. We now have hope for children living with gender identity issues that society will come to a time and place of true, loving acceptance. Our hope is contained in that love we feel for our neighbors—the ones who look and live like us and those who do not.

Is my hope an irrational one? Any fear I do harbor for Felix at times results from the recent political changes that seemingly give permission to those individuals who harbor hate and fear in their hearts to express it violently. I become dismayed when someone identifies as a person of faith yet behaves in hateful or hurtful ways. My hope comes from God, who strengthens me to stand up for children and adults alike who are moving through this type of transition.

My hope leans on the passage from Matthew 22:37–40:

> You shall love the Lord your God with all your heart, and with all your soul, and with all your mind. This is the greatest and first

commandment. And a second is like it: You shall love your neighbor as yourself. On these two commandments hang all the law and the prophets.

Nowhere in these words will you find the task of passing judgment. In society today, as in the time of Jesus, we are constantly challenged to move through the world without judgment. Many a Christian will stand and quote the Bible, stating gender variances and sexuality differences are sinful, abominations, perversions. (For fresh looks at the scriptures and what they actually say and convey with respect to sexuality issues, check out our resources guide.)

My heart and my reading of scriptures tell me that we as Christians are called to love God, ourselves, and our neighbors—not passing judgment, simply loving each other. Jesus does an excellent job of illustrating what that looks like! What it does not look like is denying someone's truth and making them afraid and anxious and unhappy. What it does not look like is subjecting our children and our peers to ridicule because of the way they are put together on the inside or the outside.

In looking more deeply into the phrase "fearfully and wonderfully made," I found references to the mysteries of God and God's creative power within us, adding a new perspective to consider. Because of the truth of these words and the loving mysteries of God, I trust God.

God has fearfully and wonderfully and mysteriously made us. God has made us capable of choosing compassion, mercy, and justice over hate, fear, and violence. We have been gifted with terrific grace! Our family and the supportive families of other transgender children are present and accounted for because of that grace. Without it, many of our families would have fallen apart. The lack of an ability to accept God's grace leaves transgender children and their families victims of fear and misunderstanding.

Unfortunately, many families of transgender children struggle with how to support their child, how to continue simply loving their child and gaining any understanding of what is happening with and to their child. Learning to lean on one's faith is vital to surviving this transition. What manner of faith tradition in which families find themselves is not so important as is the simple relationship with God we each have through prayer.

None of us knows what the next person's struggles are nor how that person has been put together. We do know the next person has as much of God in them as we do. We do know the next person is just as deserving of compassion, mercy, and understanding as we are. By accepting this belief, families can find a golden thread to hold on to while supporting and treating their child with compassion, mercy, and understanding.

I see this compassion and mercy within Felix as I hear him stand up for those who are bullied or misunderstood or treated unjustly. I understand Felix has the heart of an activist and is a seeker of justice. I trust that as he has been fearfully and wonderfully made, Felix will continue to grow into his abilities for loving kindness, seeking justice, and living in humility. These attributes are all parts of his truth—more strands of the golden thread.

I cannot number the times when I would come home from work and talk with Felix after a day at middle school and he would share some opportunity he took to educate one of his friends or other classmates about the hurtful nature of something said or done. He often called these "life lessons." I call them strands of the golden thread! When he would attend youth group at church and they would take sandwiches and hygiene kits to Little Five Points to hand out to the homeless in the area, I would often hear of how fearless he was. He would approach someone, ask if they were hungry and would like a sandwich, and then share what he had.

Quite a few years ago, a young man joined our church and during his introduction shared with the congregation that he was joining our community because when he came out as gay, his previous church had turned its back on him. Felix openly asked me why a church would do that. He was confused and dismayed. This experience definitely solidified something within Felix around inclusion and church. The topic would continue to arise over the next several months. Having to explain to such a young person that certain communities of faith had difficulty sharing God's love with everyone because of such things as their sexual orientation was heartrending for me because it was a difficult thing for me to understand as well. Yet it was also heartwarming because our church, Felix's church, is accepting.

Children easily live their truth until it is taken from them or they push it down out of fear.

Through this journey with Felix, we as a family are learning whether we are free to be as we are made. All four of us are fearfully and wonderfully made; however, are we living our truth, or have we hidden our truth? My hope and prayer is that we as Felix's family can continue providing relief, deep love, and acceptance. By exploring this together as a family, we can discover relief for the hidden parts of each our truths.

At one point not long ago, Felix confidently stood his ground around our treating him like he was Thomas. He expects us to treat him as he is—a different person than his brother in so many ways. When that conversation took place, I understood immediately. As much as we love and support Felix in his transition, we were making some assumptions about him—likes and dislikes, clothing choices, so many things. Yet when I later thought about it, why would Felix's likes and dislikes have changed simply because he was now openly living as the boy he has always been? Our assumptions conflicted with Felix's truth.

So far, this process has happened organically. I experience a greater sense of ease as well as curiosity among all of us, giving each of us permission to reach out (or in) and explore different parts of our truth. This sense of ease is also producing many moments of joy and celebration within our family!

I am constantly looking for the good in all of this; I know it exists. At times my heart seems incapable of seeing it, and sometimes I see it clearly. When I find myself struggling to see the good, I remember the following verse: "For now we see in a mirror, dimly, but then we will see face to face. Now I know only in part; then I will know fully, even as I have been fully known" (1 Cor 13:12).

Am I free from engagement with cultural and societal norms? Am I equal to the task of nurturing and empowering our child to be free and capable of love—love for himself and the way he has been made as well as love for another? All of this remains to be seen. Our journey alongside Felix is far from over, and our learning curve sometimes seems more immense than possible.

Yet because of my faith in the God within Felix and the God within each of us, I trust all will be well and good will come of this.

Questions for Consideration

1. Where in your life have you seen or experienced the golden threads of God's grace?

2. When you witness someone being mistreated or judged, what is your reaction?

3. How engaged are you with cultural and societal norms as they relate to gender?

*Bear one another's burdens, and in this way
you will fulfill the law of Christ.*

Galatians 6:2

Community:
Sharing Our Hearts,
Being Loved, Being Heard

The summer following Felix's coming out, we attended our twelfth year of a dance camp where our kids have grown up among loving, caring folks. To ease the transition at camp, we had sent messages to the planning committee and a few of our close friends who regularly attend as well. The messages were simple, loving, instructive, and educational. We shared how we hoped Felix would be received, how we were all doing with the transition, and how we hoped this year's camp would be a loving, positive experience for Felix to carry away with him. We were so pleasantly surprised to find that everyone was on point immediately! Felix heard his name and proper pronouns remarkably consistently!

I found the week an emotional roller coaster. Happy Felix was having a good experience, continuing his social transition among friends. Happy he wasn't hiding out in the cabin but instead was camped out in the dance hall drawing and presenting an intriguing presence that a lot of people wanted to be near. Sweet and loving is the experience I recall. As the week drew to a close, I had the privilege of a long talk with a good friend of mine in which I confessed all my sadness at this transition, all my concerns for Felix's future, all my whys.

My conversation with my friend is a prime example of how grief works: a loving friend and community, time spent in laughter and dancing, leading up to saying long goodbyes and sharing a powerful time with my friend. I needed that conversation as much as I have needed any other sort of support.

Each year during camp week, we have a silent auction to raise money for our camp scholarship fund. This particular year, a woman who is an incredible craftswoman brought a hand-sewn cloth doll. As soon as it came up in the auction, I leaned over to Ralph and said, "I'm getting that doll." He totally understood. With tears in my eyes, I kept lifting my paddle until the woman I was bidding against made eye contact. Apparently it was obvious I was going to keep bidding!

The doll has beautiful yarn hair in long ringlets, similar in color to Felix's. He had asked that he have a "guy" haircut for camp that year, and we had bleached his hair in anticipation of coloring it. Gone were the golden wild child braids of his youth; in was the glowing white hair waiting on the palette of colors to come. Transitions, transitions, transitions!

Now, I find it difficult to put into words why I wanted the doll so badly. Yet I realize the doll has come to represent the images in my heart of my daughter—a sort of talisman for all of those gender-specific hopes and dreams I had had for my daughter—that so many moms have for their daughters. For the first few months after coming home from camp, I admit to often weeping while looking at the doll. I tried to do so without Felix knowing it, not wanting him to feel sad.

I now know that the time I spent honestly searching my heart for all of the tendrils of daughter images, instilling them in this beautiful, tenderly made doll was time well spent. In doing that work, I was better able to accept the beautiful young man who was being revealed. The doll doesn't evoke the same emotions today as it did that summer; she sits patiently in a basket in my "she-shed," hanging out with two Beanie Baby bears and a stuffed doll that was my mother's when she was a baby.

Learning the language to use in sharing the fact of Felix's transition with members of our circle of friends and close community who knew him as our daughter has had its ups and downs. While attending Sunday services in which our son Thomas and other seniors were being recognized for graduation from high school, a lovely friend of mine, Emily, who hadn't seen Felix since he began his transition, asked where my daughter was. Felix happened to be sitting between Ralph and me. I blurted out something about our daughter having transitioned, which was met with a look of total confusion and compassion and worry on this dear woman's face. Her expression was painful to see because I immediately knew what she was thinking because of my poor word choice. I felt so unprepared for the conversation.

Later, after services were over, I found Emily and shared more clearly what was happening within our family and that our child was alive and well. Following our more revealing conversation, when Emily had the opportunity to greet Felix, she remembered and addressed him as Felix, using proper pronouns and everything. My heart swelled with happiness, hope, and love! Ever since then, she has continued to be loving and supportive to me.

First Christian Church of Decatur's acceptance of our family and Felix's journey has kept presenting itself over the past couple years. The church had the honor of hosting the wedding of our friends Paul and Billy. Watching our friends promise to love, honor, and cherish each other until death parts them was uplifting to me in a special way because of Felix. Felix's opportunity to see two men make those promises to each other showed him that his future could look that way too. I have hopes for Felix's own love and marriage one day.

With respect to the family's community transition, after my failed attempt at that quick explanation to my friend Emily, I realized it might be easier if we developed something of an "elevator speech." However, what seven to ten words could possibly encompass even a fraction of what Felix is enduring and what our family is learning in this process? For now I keep falling back on this: "Our daughter has come out to us as being transgender, so now we're happy to say we have two boys!"

Throughout this transition for Felix and for us, we have had the support of therapists, psychiatrists, doctors, and a support group—not to mention our close circle of family and friends; my faith communities of First Christian Church of Decatur as well as Sandy Springs Christian Church; and my employer, Victoria Collier. I cannot imagine moving through this without that support, which begs the question, "How could this be done alone?" The simple answer is that I don't think it could be done well or in any healthy way in isolation—for the individual transitioning nor their family.

While my faith communities and all of our faithful friends have supported us unequivocally, there are a lot of children and young adults who find themselves moving, living, and growing through this alone and unsupported by family or their faith communities. What has been a beautiful, soul healing gift (or golden thread) to our family is the realization that we do not have to move through this in isolation. There are people out there, perhaps even unbeknownst to us, who are eager to support us and our children. I was sweetly surprised by the quiet, strong support of a couple of our friends. Such is the strength of the bonds of love that have surrounded us all.

An important aspect of that support being possible is the fact that we didn't hide what our family was moving through (I'm not sure how we could have hidden it!). Yet we made sure our friends understood what was happening—truly understood—from the very beginning. This sort of openness, however, comes with a cost—that of vulnerability and trust. Each time I shared the news with friends, I admit to holding my breath and waiting for an expression or word or question. At times we were doing quite a bit of educating.

Sending Felix off to the eighth-grade semiformal dance at the end of that first year of our knowing was beautiful and sad to me. Beautiful because he found the right outfit so he felt comfortable in his own skin—probably for the first time in a long time. I have pictures of him standing in our backyard against our huge old oak (yes, that one). He has his dress shirt on, an awesome vest, a wonderful bow tie, dress pants, and shoes. Everything had been purchased in the men's department. The salesman who had assisted us was probably easily in his late 50s or early 60s. The respectful, tender way he had helped Felix brings tears to my eyes even now. I remember making eye contact with him, silently acknowledging his compassion. He understood. It was plain on his face. He respected the strength it took for Felix and for me as his mom to be out shopping for this outfit.

As this particular day drew to a close, I was a bit sad because, for me, it was yet another shift in my head and heart. These shifts, important as they are, never seem to stop coming.

Just like in labor, with each inexorable shift, Felix is being born anew into a new life. As his mother my role in this birth is again to nurture his growth and development.

Of course, a vital part of the entire picture of his growth and development has been his transition at school. An important and imposing segment of that transition for all of us was Felix's move into high school the fall following his coming out to us. While we had been working on our own transition with Felix over the previous nine months, it was time to move him and us more fully into the public eye.

This transition meant having an important strategy meeting with the principal of the high school. Our therapist accompanied Ralph and me to the meeting, bearing the gift of a binder of resources and educational information for the principal to share with his staff. During our conversation with the principal, he said, "I want to do everything I can to ensure that Felix can walk the halls of this school just like any other *young man*." My heart was full! Talk about reassurance!

We had been open with the principal regarding treatments and the commitment Felix had already shown to the transition process. I truly believe it was our openness and willingness to discuss this process and where our son was in the process that made it clear to the principal that we fully supported Felix.

Because Felix was in the early stages of transitioning, accommodations were made for his changing out for physical education by setting aside a private office for him to use. While a wonderful idea, Felix did not feel comfortable with that solution since it tended to draw attention to him as being different. Yet, undeniably, the effort to make accommodations for Felix, to keep him safe, made Ralph and me feel so much more at ease about this aspect of his social transition.

Happening at the same time were more conversations with rings of people further out from our "center." I recall having a conversation with a colleague of mine, Joe, who went through a now common litany of questions, including, "Are you sure it isn't a phase?" We had a very intense conversation about the truth of transgenderism and what it means for the person who comes to that awareness, especially after years of questioning and hiding. We also discussed what it means for the family of the person who comes to that awareness. My colleague has seen firsthand what Felix's transition has meant for our family. Almost immediately after we talked, Joe began seeing and hearing more about transgenderism—funny how that works! From that information and education, he and his wife have become prayerful supporters of our family. Their prayers are always in my heart and offer yet another thread of gold for me.

Another ring of support is that of my employer, Victoria Collier, and my teammates. Victoria won my heart when, after I shared the news, she began sending me emails with links to various articles on transgenderism and current events and medical interventions (of the good kind). Victoria continues being a supporter and advocate, which makes my days at work possible when Felix is having a difficult time. I'm safe; I'm supported—another strand of the golden thread.

Indisputably, this journey is hard for me as a mom. Often I will sit quietly in the morning sipping my coffee and question: I question my commitment;

I question doctors' treatment suggestions; I most especially question God. Even in the midst of my faithful representation of God to my child, I question why my child is having to go through this. My question to God is one I am sure resounds through most, if not all, mothers' hearts who are going through this. I know the answer to that question: if not my child, then whose? I cannot deny that Felix is not moving through this transition in isolation.

Transitioning for me and my language is ongoing. Not long ago, while having a simple conversation with a friend and Felix, I misgendered him three times in quick succession and did not hear myself. Felix got upset—rightfully so—and called me on it right then and there! Usually I hear myself and self-correct, but I didn't this time for some reason. Felix questioned me intensely in front of my friend. I was mortified because I had not heard myself. That was painful. Those words hurt me and hurt Felix. Out of all the times I have slipped up, Felix was deeply upset with me this time. I imagine it felt like I was slapping him. Overcome with sadness and frustration, I asked him to forgive me. For the first time I felt reluctance—albeit briefly—on his part to do so. That incident has made me ever so careful not to misgender him—in his presence or not. I believe perhaps that's why it happened—to solidify my language, my commitment to stop translating and simply begin thinking 100% in this new language.

Generally speaking, as Ralph and I have struggled to transition our vocabulary, Felix has continuously demonstrated much grace. I asked him about it once, and he said he knew we were trying and that's what mattered. There remain times when he holds us accountable for what he experiences as laziness, I believe. That's okay too. We need that to keep us on this path with him. We all are committed to be a part of this journey with him—another strand of the golden thread.

We have the choice of lovingly supporting Felix within the communities of our family, friends, church, and work by helping him discover the full truth of his being, teaching him healthy boundaries, as well as allowing and encouraging him to discover his place in the community and the world. We are limited in this only by our own fears, our own grief, our own need to grow and change.

In light of our own need for sustained growth and development, we will aid Felix in his. The delight and privilege of being a family is not about having all the answers ahead of time and getting this whole "raising a child" thing perfect. The delight and privilege is living and learning with each other and from each other.

Questions for Consideration

1. Identify your circles of support.

2. Have you ever revealed a situation or problem you or your family were moving through and received the graceful support of your circles? How did you experience that support?

3. Did you find God in the midst of those circles?

Great things are done by a series of small things brought together.

Vincent Van Gogh

Our attachment to our small, separate, false self must die to allow our True Self — our basic and unchangeable identity in God — to live fully and freely.

Richard Rohr

Love is patient; love is kind; love is not envious
or boastful or arrogant or rude.

⁓

It bears all things, believes all things,

hopes all things, endures all things.

⁓

And now faith, hope, and love abide,
these three;

and the greatest of these is love.

1 Corinthians 13:4, 7, 13

Process:
Loving, Listening, Learning
(and the Importance of Latin)

As much as this has been an emotional and intellectual process for Felix and our family, we cannot neglect talking about the physical part of this transition and its effects on our emotional, intellectual, and social transitioning.

When Felix uttered, "Mom, I'm a boy," one of the myriad thoughts that blew through my mind was, "What does this mean for him physically?" We soon found out!

As the physical transitioning process began, I felt myself move from my head to my heart and back to my head so often in what seems like milliseconds.

The first much-needed and eagerly anticipated purchase was that of a binder for Felix to wear in public. The entire idea of his wearing a binder to lessen the appearance of his breasts was worrisome for me. Research into the proper way and the length of time each day to wear a binder was something Felix and I did together. I totally understood the desire to do this, yet I was worried initially about the possible detrimental effects wearing one all the time would have on his body. I give Felix credit for working through his own emotions about this first step of transitioning. The time he took to learn about binding and then reason with himself to not abuse his body by wearing a binder too long in the day showed a surprising level of maturity. Felix has developed a very good awareness of when he has had the binder on too long and will do what he has to do to be able to take it off.

After a lot of psychological work with our therapist as well as his psychiatrist, in addition to beginning to move through the world as a boy socially, Felix was approved to receive hormone therapy. In Felix's case that meant he would begin receiving testosterone injections every 28 days. The dosage began at a very low level and has been slowly increasing.

A lot of deep breathing was required of me at Felix's early visit to the endocrinologist as we sat and listened to the doctor explain to Felix all the effects the testosterone would have on his body—from the lowering of his voice and formation of an "Adam's apple," to the cessation of the functioning of his ovaries.

At that point Felix was 15 years old. The endocrinologist asked him some questions I assumed would be extremely difficult for a 15-year-old to answer. I was wrong. Clearly, Felix had been considering the questions and how he felt about the answers before this appointment. Any questions about moving forward with treatment, whether he thought he would want any children, and what his thoughts were about surgeries down the road were met with confidence and a sureness I found difficult to witness. I was sitting there listening and beginning to feel overwhelmed with the details. It was one thing to intellectually "know" what this would mean to Felix's body, to his life going forward, and totally another thing to hear these changes being discussed in such a clinical way.

Please wait. Slow down. Allow my heart to catch up!

While I continue to be impressed by the growth of his confidence, Felix has not yet been willing to learn how to self-inject the testosterone, which he will need the rest of his life. This is a lesson for which Felix isn't ready!

I have stepped away and "looked" at Felix so I can see the physical changes taking place. He has now been on testosterone for more than a year, and the changes are obvious. His voice is much lower; he has an "Adam's apple," albeit a small one for now; and oh my word, he's very hairy! A recent milestone was the purchase of a razor and all the accessories. Felix shaves infrequently—more just to say he did than out of any real need.

One of the changes in Felix that has had him confused is how to "take up space" like a man. He's got it down pretty much while he's sitting, and I'm proud to say he's almost perfect with it now when he walks. I have witnessed the emotional backlash when he has been misgendered by someone in public—a salesperson, a drive-through window worker. At one point after a particularly emotional response to being misgendered in public, I suggested he watch the football players at the high school to see how they walked down the hall. Obviously, Felix has been doing a lot of reconnaissance—watching other men and learning the subtleties of walking like a man. As a result Felix is rarely misgendered in public anymore.

There have been times during this aspect of Felix's transition when I have felt like I have been moving through deep mud emotionally—being encouraging and supportive as new and different things are happening with Felix's body, yet realizing how far away from that initial "daughter" image he is unrelentingly progressing. That progress is not a bad thing; it is simply a thing I must process in both my heart and my head. The processing that I and the rest of us are doing is essential to the emotional and physical support and nurture we have available to offer our child. In order to maintain our sanity, we cannot sit back and not process what he and we are going through!

Having a strong faith in God's presence has helped me with my processing as I sit with my emotions as well as my desire to support Felix. Prayer and meditation help me keep things in balance. I am free to experience my emotions, of course, and I do; yet being able to maintain such a balance between my own emotions and my desire to nurture aids in helping keep Felix steady as he moves through his own emotions and needs for nurture. As a typical teenager his needs for nurture look a lot different than they did when he was younger! More time simply being present seems to be the ticket at this point.

Early on, Ralph, Felix, and I had a huge argument about the name "Felix." Ralph and I simply did not understand the defiant nature of his unwillingness to even consider another name. As a result the three of us ended up at the therapist's office to have her act as a mediator. I was grieving the loss of the name that tied my child to some small bit of my family history. In addition to being the product of nine months of thought, concern, and negotiation, Felix's birth name carried my maternal grandmother's middle name. Felix had chosen this name in seventh grade! Of course, at that point we had no idea of his transgender status and thus had absolutely no input.

Beautifully, the emotionally charged conversation led to an understanding on Felix's part of the importance we had placed on naming our children.

Just as beautifully, the conversation also allowed us an understanding of why "Felix" was heartfelt and true for him. We learned that "Felix" derives from Latin and means "lucky, successful, happy"—all very important attributes for our son.

We understood more; he understood more— another strand of that golden thread.

As I prepared the petition to change my child's name, I wept—not some gentle weeping, but lots of tears streaming down my face. Filling the paperwork out was physically challenging; my body was resistant to doing the work. Filing the paperwork at the courthouse was in an odd way embarrassing; only now do I realize that emotion rose from a place of denial so deep as to be unidentifiable as such. Yet after about six weeks, when the order came through, I was able to celebrate with Felix authentically that first legal step.

Grief found me again as I waited at the window to change his birth certificate. On a whim and a hope, I asked the clerk whether I could also change the gender. The clerk asked me if there had been a mistake at birth. Even though the clerk had asked in a noncommittal, nonjudgmental way, that question punched me hard and left tears piling up behind my eyes.

"Yes...no...I don't know," I stammered.

Oh, the conversation that was happening in my head. The clerk just stared at me, waiting for my answer.

After what seemed to me to be an interminable delay, I said, "No."

Strictly speaking, as far as we had known then, there had been no mistake. Anger seeped in when I realized that society had only given us two boxes. Knowing what I knew standing there at that window, I wondered why we had been made to mark one at all.

Since I had answered "no" to the question of some mistake at birth, the clerk informed me I would need to have the final order for name change amended to reflect an appropriate change in gender marker. I immediately wished I could have rewound our conversation and answered "yes." I have often wondered what the clerk's answer or reaction would have been. Nevertheless, I left the window feeling defeated. When I reached the car, I sat there and sobbed until I was ready and willing to accept the comfort and grace God was offering—another strand of the golden thread.

We were granted an amended birth certificate reflecting Felix's new name but same gender. I remember the sweet anguish I felt when I opened the envelope containing the new birth certificate. Sweet because it was one more accomplishment on Felix's behalf. Anguish because it was one more step away from what was. As soon as we could, Felix and I took it to the school records office. The clerk there was gently supportive and affirming. She submitted the birth certificate without marking the gender, leaving it blank and saying that was how she had been doing it for a while. We knew then that Felix wasn't the trailblazer we had thought he would have been!

Throughout ninth grade, even without the birth certificate having been changed, the high school had been supportive. Felix and I put together a letter containing, in his own words, an explanation of where he was in his transition as well as a photo. In addition to Felix handing this letter to each teacher the first day of class, the counseling office had marked "Felix" as the preferred name on his records. When he came home from school that first day, he was exhausted, but I was so very proud of his determination to take one more step on this path.

All in all, Felix experienced quite a high degree of support from the teaching staff—with one glaring exception. The exception was a surprise after all the great support we had received. By the beginning of the second semester, I had to inform the principal that a particular teacher was carelessly and perhaps even intentionally being uncooperative and sabotaging Felix's social transition by being inconsistent with the use of Felix's preferred name (all over the classroom records) as well as his preferred gender. The principal immediately set a meeting with the teacher and me. The teacher denied he was doing so intentionally, using the excuse that he saw "so many kids" during the day. I reminded him that all of Felix's other teachers were on board since the first day of school, and they saw at least as many, if not more, students than he did in a day. I also warned him that if he didn't stop, I would bring a suit against him under Title IX. The principal was listening intently at this point and assured me the teacher would be more consistent and careful. I responded that he had better be. On any occasion where I found myself advocating for Felix, "Mama Bear" was just under the surface.

Tenth grade started off with Felix's name being the only name on the records now that we had submitted the changed birth certificate. We were excited!!

Changing Felix's name with our health insurance company had been surprisingly easy. Imagine that! I just had to send in the final order for name change. I have been truly surprised by the reaction of Blue Cross Blue Shield of Georgia around the payment of medical expenses associated with doctors' visits and medical treatments. Since going to our first appointment with the endocrinologist, Felix has had an official diagnosis of "transgenderism." Apparently that magic word has opened the door with the insurance company!

Sitting down with the clerk at the Social Security office was both an educational and a compassionate experience. I was given information about a letter Felix's endocrinologist could write that would make it possible for the gender marker on Felix's record with SSA to be altered. The young man who was helping me took at least half an hour working with his supervisor to find the information we needed. I left feeling very supported and recognized for the work I was doing on behalf of my child. I am always amazed at the palpability of God's presence in these situations. Compassion, love, and understanding were always present in the entire conversation with this clerk. He was truly desirous of helping me help my son. Needless to say, I was touched by the time and attention he offered me—grace-filled golden threads!

Informing our church was not a big deal in and of itself. First Christian Church of Decatur, while not officially so at the time, has been open and welcoming as far as the LGBTQ community is concerned for as long as I have been a member. As a side note, at the time I am writing this, First Christian Church of Decatur is in the early stages of officially becoming an "open and affirming" congregation. I'm proud to be a part of the core committee helping to educate and lead the congregation toward this goal.

When I hear of adults who slam the idea of transgenderism as being a sickness, a stage, or even a fad, I get angry. I get angry because I see the commitment of my child to moving through this in a healthy, consistent, way. The recent hubbub from parents who are outraged at the idea that a transgender student be allowed to use the bathroom assigned to the gender with which they identify truly infuriates me. I wonder if any of those who are speaking out against fair treatment of transgender students have ever spoken with a transgender student or with the youth's parents. I see this knee-jerk fear of something different one of the basic reasons for our society refusing to recognize the humanity of our transgender brothers and sisters.

Until we resolve to love—simply love—those we know who are moving through such a transition as this, the much-touted suicide rate among transgender folk will not decrease. This process is emotionally, intellectually, and physically demanding. Youth and adults need love and understanding as they move through the process. The suicide rate is pushed up as a direct result of the effect of mistreatment, abandonment, and abuse of transgender youth and adults. Add to that the additional discrimination and mistreatment of those transgender folk who are also non-white. All of a sudden, the rates of loss due to suicide do not seem too out of the realm of understanding!

In each of these instances, it is the love of God, the grace of God channeled through the parents, that can ease the pain a child is suffering, can make it possible to support a child as that child builds a life. As a parent I see my primary job in this journey as channeling God's grace for Felix so he knows he is loved—not just by his family, but intimately and infinitely by God—another strand of the golden thread.

Being present to and with a child is just that— staying put, being ready to act if needed, or staying watchful if no action is required. Because we have not had any idea how to move through this transition with Felix, we have done a lot of watching and waiting to determine the next thing to do that will most nurture his transition. We have also spent time pondering and listening in many respects so that our hearts can catch up with what we know in our heads. Our own thinking time is important because it allows us to reach deep into our hearts to grab those golden threads! In the lives of our children, I have found out that watching and waiting is a good thing—leaving time for them to ponder as well.

Love. Simply love. That is the answer to so many questions and worries and fears with respect to the fact of transgenderism. Love, then listen.

Grief:
Holding On to Ropes of Gold

About twelve years ago I began intensive journaling and have kept it up as a spiritual practice. Journaling for me is also a way of keeping my sanity as I have moved through various tough situations. Oddly enough, however, I have found as I move through times of difficulty with Felix, I am almost afraid to journal. Fear seizes my heart at times because I question myself—and God. Questioning God has never been a fearful or difficult interaction for me! Questions, I know, are not unusual when life is in a period of disorientation. However, even as things have smoothed out a bit and life seems to be reorienting, I still find it difficult. As I write this, I move through times of weepiness. Those times creep up on me. I believe it's because of grieving.

Grieving takes and makes its own time, rising up in unusual and unexpected ways.

Felix doesn't exactly understand what I'm grieving. After all, he understands himself as being the same person he was before he came out. I have attempted to explain to him that while he may feel he is the same, he is not experienced as being the same simply because of the fact of his coming out. The strength and courage it took to make that pronouncement changed him in a basic sort of way. A good way. I see him already maturing into that strength and courage. Not to say that he hasn't always been courageous, considering those "wild child" days with all the braids, never stopping to consider what anyone else would say or think, simply being who he is.

When I think of "being who he is," I think of the time when he was three and came with me to Wolf Photo to pick up some pictures. I'm standing there at the counter perusing my photos, oblivious to the fact that Felix had wandered from my side when a sweet little lady came up to me and touched me on the shoulder. I turned around and found her smiling broadly at me. She asked, "Are you the mother of the precious child at the front of the store?" I immediately had a sinking feeling. Really. "Precious child?" That couldn't be good. When I looked for my precious child, I saw a naked child running around the store looking at stuff. This sweet lady had been sitting with her husband in their car just outside the store when they saw this child begin taking clothes off and putting them in a neat pile— all the child's clothes—and running back and forth across the front of the store looking at merchandise. The woman said, "I just had to find the mother of this child to congratulate her on raising a child with such enthusiasm and free spirit!" I laughed out loud! Yup. That's my child.

Body issues never appeared to be an issue for Felix, at least until adolescence. I had trouble keeping clothes on that little body! Because of my own upbringing in an atmosphere of imposed modesty and body shame, I was proud of my little "show-off" in a way—or at least proud that I apparently was not passing on my own ambivalent feelings about my body. I thought that was an important aspect to parenting a daughter. I have since learned boys suffer from body image problems as often as girls but are rarely seen in the same light.

Courage and grace.

If I could write a song, it would be about that. Courage and grace. Without both of those gifts, Felix wouldn't be here. Felix had to have courage and grace to finally find his voice and speak his truth. My husband and I had to have courage and grace to step onto this path with our child and walk with him. His brother, Thomas, had to have courage and grace to make this transition and support his brother—which he has done beautifully. Thomas's friends, too, have been very supportive and accepting, whether they knew Felix before or are unaware of the transition.

Of course, I'm not sure if anyone other than me considers that the courage and grace come from God. I recognize my role in this transition partly as a spiritual resource or touchstone for the rest of my family. As I pause throughout our days and watch what this transition has done to us as individuals and as a family, I am actually pleased. So often families fall apart when something like this happens. I believe it is our awareness of God's presence—conscious or not—that enables us to hold our family together. Holding our family together is an obvious sign of a rope made from those golden threads!

As part of reflecting on Felix's development throughout his transition, I've thought a lot about the characteristics Felix has shown since birth. Were they particularly girly? Boyish? No, they were quite simply reflective of a lust for life and experiences, tempered by curiosity, kindness, mercy, compassion, humor, joy, intelligence, thoughtfulness, consideration, creativity, and a sense of justice and equality. The number of these characteristics matching the gifts of the Spirit and the qualities we are called to live according to Micah 6:8 amazes me. Although, if we're honest, most children are born with these characteristics! Having all of these is a large part of my wondering at times why it took so long for him to find his voice around his gender identity. I realize how strange it may sound, but this wondering will still occasionally bring on a time of grieving for me.

During the early days of my grieving process over Felix's transition, I found that I began to blow out of proportion the least little "failure" I perceived on my part. I was somehow supposed to be the perfect mother now that I had this child who was going through this tremendous transition. I had to be strong, good, and perfect to help him in the best way I could. Consistent with many caregivers I have known, I finally figured out that I felt that way because I never admitted to anyone—Ralph or my therapist—that I felt stupid, dumb, and unobservant. There are times, in the throes of my grief, I have experienced feelings of guilt so strong I have been convinced that I alone have made this transition more difficult than it has had to be. The effect of this deep grief and guilt is that my faith feels undone, my prayers feel empty, my efforts at reaching out to God, to Ralph, to friends—and even to some extent my therapist—failed to communicate just how badly I was feeling. From some distance now these feelings have always been indicators of trouble for me!

In the midst of all this guilt and grief, and at my therapist's suggestion, I went to my doctor and told him I thought I was depressed. He asked me why. I gave him a list I had made the night before, which was a full page of things that had happened in my life over the previous decade—decisions, events, happenings that impacted me in sometimes strong ways and sometimes subtle ways. Nevertheless, each of those events could be considered losses of some sort. He looked up occasionally while reading the entire list, seeking out my eyes. After a brief conversation, not without some amount of humor from the doctor, he diagnosed me as clinically depressed and prescribed an antidepressant.

I am glad to say that now when I fall into the grief and guilt trap, I recognize it for what it is: a lack of perspective or perhaps a lack of rest and respite. My prayers are more effective for my own heart and soul, and I definitely have more perspective on my part in Felix's transition. My "recovery" within my depression is a great part of why I am writing this book. Being depressed and grieving are two different animals. Yet when you are depressed, grieving adopts a different depth and certainly complicates your understanding of what is happening. Grieving still sneaks up on me.

Along with all the transitions for Felix, a major change to my perception of my own identity is a personal transition. Who am I now? As my kids were growing up, I was known as mom. As they aged, I gained an identity as my mother's caregiver. Following my mother's death, I discovered another identity—that of a faith-filled scholar, minister, and director of a spiritual support ministry for caregivers. Eventually, I reluctantly left my volunteer work at church to work in a law firm. My initial position there led to my current role as an estate planning paralegal. It is in my role of paralegal that I find so much beauty in the vulnerable moments I am invited to witness in the lives of our clients.

My identity as a minister has had an outlet in the spiritual support I am allowed to offer our clients as they move through a sometimes very emotional and difficult process. The identity of minister has been a part of me as long or perhaps longer than that of being someone's mom. In simplest terms the mom and the minister are the bases of who I am.

With Felix's transition I have assumed a slightly reoriented role—that of mother to a transgender child. That role brings with it an awesome responsibility also to be an advocate for other children who are moving through this transition as well as for their families. Not everyone gives credence to this transition as being one of the entire family. What I have noticed is that those families who are more open to their children exploring all of the beautiful complexity of who they are tend to be more accepting when their child comes out as gay or lesbian or bisexual, transgender, or questioning. The pain I witness within families who are not open to their children's exploration of their sexuality and gender is intense and divisive. The divisiveness reveals itself in the emotional—and sometimes physical—abandonment of their children. The family simply refuses to accept the transition their children are moving through. The damage to these children, and their families, while not irreparable, is certainly dependent upon accepting the grace that God so abundantly provides!

As a spiritual director I have made a commitment to sit with those who are transitioning as well as those mothers or fathers who are struggling with understanding what is happening with their child and within their family.

Also important has been the realization that not everyone allows mothers or fathers finding themselves in the throes of such a transition with their child the opportunity to vent. While our family has been involved with a transgender parent support group, I was eager to talk with a ministerial colleague about my experience as Felix's mom and the toll it was taking. I was taken aback by his lack of support. Given the ministry he undertakes, I was wounded by his obvious lack of compassion for what I was going through right then. How he could have had no understanding of the loving support and nurture we were offering our child still stumps me. I share this encounter and its aftermath for the single reason of illustrating that even those involved with the LGBTQ community are not always supportive of the parents who are moving through this transition with their child. Having given this episode a lot of thought, my only understanding is that perhaps he was so focused on Felix's needs that my own were not of concern.

This struggle of not being allowed to voice my own emotional exhaustion, my own desires to have my life take a different road, is, I imagine, similar to how parents often shut down their children who come to them with their feelings of dysphoria. Once again, a soapbox is never far from my feet when I'm discussing this issue with others because I can hear my own experience of the lack of compassion and empathy ringing in my ears. I now have others who do spiritually support me in a compassionate and understanding manner.

Questions for Consideration

1. What grief has you in its grips?

2. Are you calling upon God and your circles of support for assistance? For help in processing your grief?

3. Could you be a compassionate listener to someone who came to you with their own story of parenting a transgender child—or even being transgender themselves?

Again Jesus spoke to them, saying,
"I am the light of the world. Whoever follows
me will never walk in darkness but will have
the light of life."

John 8:12

Light

Thirty years ago, I held very different beliefs around homosexuality and same-sex marriage. Transgenderism was not even on the horizon as far as my experience and knowledge was concerned. I would, however, evolve.

My beliefs around such topics had been forged within a very conservative Presbyterian family. Even after leaving home, for a time I superficially held on to the beliefs I had been taught within my family; it was safer to do so initially than to seek out spiritual support and formation and form my own beliefs. I had been taught that homosexuality was evil. Period. Never to be accepted. Nor should I ever willingly associate with a homosexual. Accordingly, as I moved into the big wide world and came into contact with anyone I thought could possibly fit into that definition, I would push them away and not engage. I would, however, observe.

Same-sex marriage did not appear on my parents' radar either at the time I was growing up. Yet the idea (the hope) had begun circulating in society and began being discussed in wider circles. I pushed that away too. I would, however, listen.

I held on to these beliefs for at least a decade after leaving home. I pushed away good people, people who cared about me, people who worried about a 19-year-old living on her own in Atlanta in 1980.

Yet because I stopped to notice how the world worked, how God was moving in the world, how God was moving in me, and how I might be a part of those movements, my own ideas about love and light and relationships between people changed. My own ideas, my own theology, have developed since I left home and lived in the world—and practiced my faith in prayer, worship, and study.

I made my share of bad decisions within my own relationships by being someone who judged first and listened last. Fortunately, I have been blessed with friends who knew how to practice forgiveness. Those very mistakes and the grace I experienced from the people I judged helped shape my understanding of God. My faith was shaped by my upbringing; however, my spiritual formation did not stop there.

The first two law firms in which I worked were either owned by Jewish individuals or there were Jewish individuals in the office with whom I worked. My theology was tested and questioned and illuminated by many conversations late into the evening with my Jewish colleagues. I began to see how pervasive the love of God was in my life, in their lives, and in the world in general. This knowledge was a turning point in my spiritual development.

After my husband and I married and both of his parents had died, his brother came out to the family as gay. No one was really surprised—at least none of his siblings were. I knew and loved Ralph's brother. He was not evil. He was not anyone I wanted to avoid. I also knew him as a good and compassionate man. This was another turning point in my spiritual development.

After years of staying away from church due to confusion in my heart and spirit and not understanding how I could deal with that, I began to pray again. I had always had an intimate relationship with God and had always prayed. I had only stopped because of reaching a deep chasm with seemingly no way of crossing. My faith, however, proved that God would help me span that chasm. I slowly began hearing God's word for me through everything else but prayer. The final "word" was found within Jan Karon's *Mitford* series and particularly through her character Father Tim, who prayed constantly! As I slowly began praying, I began recognizing the holy 2 x 4s as they hit my head. As a result of those 2 x 4s, I began shaking my fist at God, then crying with God, then asking God why, then simply listening. As I prayed, I began to see things differently in the world.

As I moved through the world, I saw how people whom I was sure God loved were being hated because of who they loved. That made absolutely no sense to me. I prayed some more. I began to see even more. I began to see those people around me who were supportive of gays and lesbians in their longing to have family, to have love, in their lives.

At the time of my mother's death, I was introduced to the pastor of First Christian Church of Decatur, Rev. Dr. James Brewer-Calvert, when he came to my mother's hospital room, listened to my story, bore witness to my last words to my mother, and shared Communion. Even in the midst of my grief and my questioning, the Holy Spirit had seen to it that I come into contact with a healing, loving, and generous community of faith. This wonderful community of faith has held me as I journeyed more deeply and intentionally toward God. One of the holy 2 x 4s that has recently hit me concerns the "knowing" that God has of our needs, our desires, our pasts, our futures.

Almost a decade ago, I began a program at Columbia Theological Seminary in Decatur, Georgia, titled "Certificate in Spiritual Formation." This program had been developed to give those who attended the formation, the training, and the tools to guide others in the formation of their faith. What an eye- and ear- and heart-opening experience! Through this program I learned a new way of looking, seeing, and learning—a way that blew open my heart. I was thankful I had the support of the community at First Christian Church of Decatur!

By prayer, study, and worship I have taken on a new language of faith and have decided to hunker down with my child for the long run.

I know I have God with me. I know each time I am shown something I don't understand, if I fall back on what I know of God's love, it's much easier to cope with, to learn from, and to accept the change.

All of this is not to say that I/we don't have rules that we follow both in our family and in our community. It is to say that before I react with a lack of understanding, I do my best to default to a place of love.

I still receive the occasional well-placed holy 2 x 4 and will be forced to admit to having been judgmental or unkind or having jumped ahead of God's timing. As this journey with Felix continues, I remain impatient at times. Why that impatience rears its head at particular times puzzles me. I believe it's because, as usual, I have wanted to know, to see further than God has wanted me to see. So as Felix continues his transition, coming into his own, becoming such a wonderful young man, and showing the confidence I have been eager to see, I remain impatient with myself, with the occasional slips of pronouns. I continue to question myself!

Why? The answer remains in my own transition. My transition includes changes in the way in which I see my child. I now see Felix as a deeply thoughtful young man. My transition includes letting go of any expectations I have for Felix's life. Actually, that transition, that letting go of expectations, applies to both my boys. It only makes sense. Instead of planning their lives for them, in my head or otherwise, I have learned they are completely capable of planning their own. I have begun to trust and rely upon what Ralph often tells me: "They will figure it out. Just give them time," he says.

I will give them time; I will also give them my love, then listen.

Questions for Consideration

1. Have your beliefs changed over your lifetime?

2. How would you describe the process?

3. How would you describe God's presence in the process?

Conclusion?
Not Yet!

I have no way of knowing what the rest of Felix's life holds for him. I pray every day that he will be safe. Of course, I pray that for my son Thomas every day as well. I believe every mother has that prayer tattooed on her heart. I do know, as a matter of faith, that God is with Felix—both in this transition and in all other parts of his life.

The transition of my son has influenced how I look at myself. I see myself through a different lens now—a lens of deep love and faith, a lens of desire to bear witness to the journey of a child, a lens of forgiveness—of myself and others for not "getting it," for missing the cues. There's also a very large lens of grace through which I see my parenting, our family, and especially our son Felix.

The grief I have experienced is transitioning my own soul. This grief has hewn from this journey a new strength, a new confidence in God's grace and God's presence in not only my life, but also that of my family.

Our family continues to live our life together on multiple fronts: in a loving community, a weird in-between place, and a place of having to take a stand. As our journey continues, so does our education in how to move among these fronts. We are fortunate to have a tremendous community of friends, family, and faith that we trust to take us where they find us.

The weird in-between place is a large part of the reason I'm writing this book. I am drawn to offer myself to others I know who are moving through transitions—offering emotional support, spiritual direction, and simple presence. I strive to offer a way of seeing God in this transition. God has a beautiful way of working in the world—through drawing us to a life of loving kindness, seeking justice, and moving, living, and being in humility.

What about taking a stand? Well, my soap box is never far from my feet. My husband and I still come into contact with friends and family who are shocked by our son's transition and speak against it. Taking a stand is difficult for our entire family. Yet we do so because we love our child.

Taking a stand is incumbent upon me because God has also called me to speak out and to give a voice to those who are struggling, alone, and fearful—including families struggling to discern how to love and support a child.

I praise you, for I am fearfully and
wonderfully made.

Wonderful are your works;
that I know very well.

~

When I awake, I am still with you.

(Psalm 139:14, 18b)

What Worked and Didn't Work for Our Family

My aim in sharing the information contained in the next few pages is to provide my readers with information I did not have at the outset and now wish I had. I will be offering suggestions on various topics—from informing family and friends to praying and meditating, and a lot in between.

I remember thinking, "Why is this happening to us?" When I could breathe again, what came to me was that we were not alone in moving through this with our child. There were so many other families who had trod this path before us. Also, I learned to accept that my faith is sufficient for this journey. I urge you to believe that of your own faith. Your child being transgender is not something God is doing to you or your child. In fact, God is walking this path with your entire family. Praying, journaling, and sitting in silence (crying is good too), listening for God's comfort and solace are your greatest tools for moving through this with grace.

Another great tool for my husband and I has been dance—contra dance to be exact. Friday nights. So if you and your family have a regular physical outlet for frustrations of the week at work or whatever, keep that in your life.

When you get past a lot of your shock and hesitation, ask your child, "Will you please tell me your story? I want to hear you; I want to truly listen to you." Your child may take a while to start— minutes, hours, days, or even weeks; give them that space—yet when they begin, listen. Listen with an open heart; weep openly—it's okay. If your child becomes upset that you're crying, reassure them and ask that they keep talking. You may even be able to say that you are weeping for them, for the struggle they have endured up to this point; you're weeping in gratitude that they are sharing with you, that they are indeed still present—if you say anything, make sure it is your truth. Once they share their truth with you, be trustworthy with it. Never use anything they shared against them. Take it, and as Mary did, ponder it in your heart.

Telling others should always be a decision reached first by your child and then agreed upon by the immediate family. Sharing often begins with family members who are not living with you, although sometimes the first ones to know are close friends. Once you do tell someone, give them some space to digest it all. Do ask for their discretion in sharing the information with others; explain that it is your child's decision when and with whom to share their news. The space and time you allow is time for you and your child to figure out your next move. I know that sounds calculating; however, strategy is important at this point.

Telling folks willy-nilly can backfire when you have forgotten whom you've told and whom you haven't. Have a plan.

When you do share the news with someone, keep it simple. There is no reason to beat around the bush. There will undoubtedly be questions and/or comments.

Some simple suggestions would be:

"Our daughter Susan has come out to us as transgender. So we now have a son, Samuel, to love and see grow into a strong, determined young man. We are proud of him. We hope you will be too."

"Our son Alex has come to us and shared that he is gender nonconforming and is listening and learning more about how he perceives his gender. For now Alex would prefer to have the pronouns 'they, them, and their' used when speaking with them."

Personally, I have found this to be very difficult; Felix has a good friend who is gender nonconforming and chooses to use "they, them, and their." It has taken a long time to adjust to those pronouns. In this example "Alex" has retained a male-sounding name, yet there are female "Alex" folks out there too. Trying to explain what this means is difficult—give yourself space and grace in doing so. It is okay to admit the difficulty and yet still communicate the expectation of support and acceptance.

Remember, gender is experienced along a spectrum and is not simply male or female. Some individuals are actually gender-fluid, never knowing how they might wake up experiencing themselves. I simply cannot imagine a more difficult life. So when someone shares such a truth and shares the pronouns he/she/they need/want to hear used, do your best to oblige them.

There is immense courage required of anyone who comes out as transgender—wherever they fall on that spectrum. Respect, acceptance, love—the same qualities we all seek in our lives—are sought by transgender individuals.

Our journey with Felix has been covered in prayer from the outset. I believe we would not be where we are now if we had not been on the receiving end of so many prayers. My own time spent in prayer and in listening for God's word and grace has been fruitful. So what comes next are some spiritual support and formation resources that I have depended upon greatly. I encourage you to explore!

Resources for Spiritual Support and Formation

In Times of Caregiving: Prayers of Renewal & Restoration by Robert M. Hamma [This book is a personal favorite of mine and is chock-full of prayers, short readings, meditations—all for the caregiver. Remember, you are your child's caregiver in this.]

Psalms for Young Children by Marie-Hélène Delval [Yes, I know. It is a book for "young children." However, the author catches the essential emotions of each psalm—check out Psalm 139.]

Psalms for Praying: An Invitation to Wholeness by Nan C. Merrill [Another longtime favorite. Merrill, in her preface to the 10th anniversary edition states, "To pray is to be transformed.... May the prayers of all who read, pray, or sing the Psalms help awaken us to the Peace of the Beloved indwelling in every soul."]

Finding God: Praying the Psalms in Times of Depression by Thomas Lewis [I share within this book that I live with depression, that I sought out help after being encouraged by my therapist. I realize not everyone reading this book will have a therapist. However, I plead with you to seek help if you find yourself in a pervasive dark place. It is my heartfelt belief that God does not want us to languish in such a place. Learn its lessons, and move through. This small book helped me tremendously in doing just that.]

The Cup of Our Life: A Guide to Spiritual Growth by Joyce Rupp, OSM [I've used this one over and over as a personal devotional through different seasons of my life, always coming away with fresh insights and deeper awareness.]

Little Pieces of Light...Darkness & Personal Growth by Joyce Rupp, OSM [Another powerful little book.]

Forgiving Your Family: A Journey to Healing by Kathleen Fischer [When faced with my own family history of hurt and betrayal, working through this particular book was lifesaving for me and brought a new awareness of the condition of my own soul.]

This I Know: A Simple Biblical Defense for LGBTQ Christians by Jim Dant [A perfect little book to carry around with you for quick reference!]

Changing Our Mind: Definitive Edition of the Landmark Call for Inclusion of LGBT Christians with Response to Critics by David P. Gushee

Resources

TransThriving

TransThriving is a therapeutic wellness program for gender-diverse youth and their families. They created an environment built out of love and compassion for all. The goal at TransThriving is to provide a safe space where gender-diverse youth can be open and explore their authentic self. TransThriving's wraparound approach provides support to the entire family as they navigate this sometimes perplexing, unique path. This specific program and team provides clinical support services tailored to the individual needs by reassuring the clients that they are not alone and are worthy of leading happy, healthy, and thriving lives.

Call: 404-257-6757

Email: thrive@thrivingheart.com

Website: transthriving.com

The Trevor Project

The Trevor Project is known to be "the leading national organization providing crisis intervention and suicide prevention services to lesbian, gay, bisexual, transgender, and questioning (LGBTQ) young people ages 13–24." This organization offers programs and services geared for the LGBTQ youth community. They provide trainings and resources to help educate and aid communities, schools, volunteers, and individuals. The Trevor Project provides support and resources for youth and their allies to help prevent suicide. For more information or help please call or text 1-866-488-7386.

Email: info@thetrevorproject.com

Website: thetrevorproject.com

*Becoming Nicole: The Transformation of
an American Family* by Amy Ellis Nutt;
https://www.amazon.com/Becoming-
Nicole-Transformation-American-Family/
dp/0812995430

*Stuck in the Middle with You: A Memoir of Parenting
in Three Genders* by Jennifer Finney Boylan

*Now What? A Handbook for Families
with Transgender Children* by Rex Butt;
https://www.amazon.com/Now-What-
Handbook-Families-Transgender/
dp/0986084417

*The Transgender Child: A Handbook for Families
and Professionals* by Stephanie A. Brill, Rachel
Pepper; https://www.barnesandnoble.com/w/
transgender-child-stephanie-a-brill/1110898127

*The Transgender Teen: A Handbook for Parents and
Professionals Supporting Transgender and Non-Binary
Teens* by Stephanie A. Brill and Lisa Kenney; https://
researchpress.com/books/1375/transgender-teen

CPSIA information can be obtained
at www.ICGtesting.com
Printed in the USA
LVOW13s1052290518
578827LV00033B/582/P